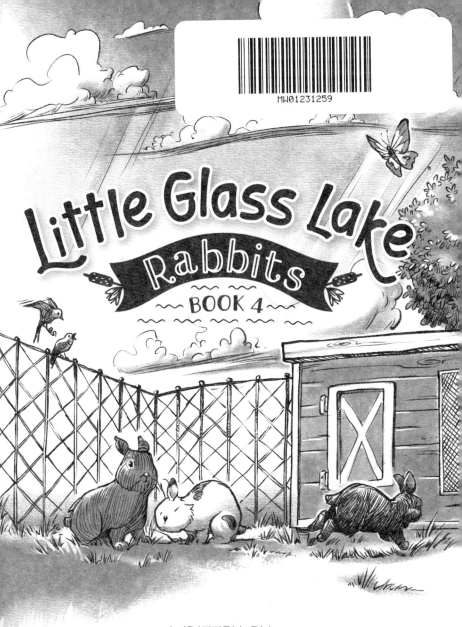

Little Glass Lake Rabbits

BOOK 4

WRITTEN BY

Jenny Phillips

ILLUSTRATED BY

Brandon Dorman

TABLE OF CONTENTS

Chapter 1

When Holly woke up one hot, breezy summer morning, she had no idea how exciting the day would be.

She wore her favorite overalls, and, as always, her mom braided blue ribbons into her hair.

Every morning while

Holly's hair was being braided, her mom told her a Bible story.

This morning, Holly's mom recounted a story Jesus once told—a parable. A shepherd had one hundred sheep, and one went missing. The shepherd left the ninety-nine sheep to search hard and long for

that one missing sheep.
Of course, this story
made Holly want to go see
the sheep farm ten miles

away from her home. Henry, who had just turned fifteen, had taken Holly there once before on their bikes. Nice bike trails ran alongside the road. They could make it to the sheep farm in less than two hours. It was far, so they didn't bike there often.

"After your chores you can go if Henry will take

you," Mom said. "It will take you a lot of the day, but we don't have plans, so it's a great day to go!"

Henry loved the sheep farm too, and he said he would take Holly there.

A lovely blue sky looked down on two very happy siblings as they tightened their helmets, hopped on their bikes, and headed down the lane.

First, they went through what Holly called the Tree Tunnel, which was a stretch of road to the left of their house that had great, twisting trees lining each side of the road. The high branches arched over the road and formed a shady, leafy green tunnel.

Holly wiped her brow, noting what a hot day it was. As they rode along, she watched two squirrels chasing each other up a tree and listened to the wind rush through thousands of leaves above her.

Something on the side of the road caught her eye—a sign she had never seen before. She read it and skidded to a stop.

"Wait, Henry! Come here!" Holly yelled.

Henry turned his bike and rode back to where Holly was standing.

"Look!" Holly gasped. "This sign says 'For Sale.' Is someone selling the Tree Tunnel?"

Henry studied the big

sign. "It has a map on it," he explained. "It looks like there is a large section of property between Gabe's house and our house that is being sold!"

"But I thought Gabe's family owned that land," Holly wondered.

"I think they do," Henry answered. He called their mom on his

new phone watch and
asked if they could go talk
to Gabe before going to
the sheep farm.

Gabe was doing chores, so he couldn't talk long, but he explained that his family was selling that part of their land.

"My dad's old truck finally died, and he needs to buy another one. Also, our potato crop failed. The potatoes got a disease, and we won't have any potatoes to sell this

year. Dad has decided
not to have a potato field
anymore. His brother
has asked him to come
work with him. We need
the money, so we are
selling half of our land. I
guess we'll both have new
neighbors. Whoever buys
the land will probably
build a house on it."

New neighbors, Holly

thought as she and Henry continued their bike ride to the sheep farm.

I don't think I want new neighbors. Their house will be even closer to mine than Faith's and Gabe's houses. But I also feel bad for Gabe's family. They've been having a hard time.

Holly and Henry had one more mile to the

sheep farm. Not many people lived in this area. As the siblings rode their bikes, Holly noticed that the wind had picked up.

Huge oak trees stood here and there in the fields, and their big branches swayed back and forth. The long golden grass rippled like ocean waves.

Holly sniffed. *It smells like smoke,* she thought with a little twinge of worry.

Chapter 2

Slowing down his bike, Henry pulled alongside Holly. "Hey, do you smell smoke?"

"Yes, and the smell seems to be getting stronger," Holly noted.

The two stopped their bikes and looked around. Holly noticed a cloud of smoke rising above a forest of trees ahead of them.

"Look over there," Henry said, pointing at the smoke.

"Maybe it's a farmer burning some weeds," Holly said.

"Maybe," Henry replied. "Let's keep going."

They started riding

toward the sheep farm again. As they rounded a bend in the road, the siblings skidded their bikes to a stop.

The field of golden grass in front of them was on fire. The fire was not large, and no trees were burning, but the

wind was pushing the hungry fire around the field rapidly, and already several bushes had caught fire.

Holly's heart pounded in her chest. *This is a real emergency!*

"Should we try to put it out?" Holly called to Henry.

"Definitely not," Henry

responded. "It would not be safe. But we need to get help right away. I doubt anyone else knows that the fire has started. And this wind is making the fire spread fast."

Holly looked around. "Mr. Juggins's bee farm is very close—just around the next bend. Should we go tell him?"

"Yes, but first I need to call 911!" Henry exclaimed. "We can ride to Mr. Juggins's house afterward. Yikes! Look how fast the fire is spreading!"

"Good idea! Hurry! I'm so glad you thought of calling 911."

Henry took a deep breath and touched the

numbers on his watch. "This is scary! But I have to do it."

Holly's heartbeat raced as she listened to the 911 dispatcher's voice asking Henry for his location.

A little panicked, Henry looked around. "I . . . I don't know exactly," he stuttered. Then he took a deep breath again to calm himself. "We are on Oak Hollow Road near Mr. Juggins's bee farm."

It was a little hard to hear the dispatcher because it was so windy, but they listened carefully.

"Emergency vehicles will be arriving soon. Leave the area now and get to a safe place," the dispatcher continued.

"Thank you for notifying us. That was the right thing to do!"

"Oh no!" Holly exclaimed, pointing to the huge plumes of dark smoke rising from the field. "Look, the big oak tree in the middle of the field has caught on fire, and the tree over there is on fire too! The wind is making this fire explode!"

"The fire is spreading fast and catching trees on fire," Henry explained to the dispatcher on the line. "The wind is pushing the fire away from us, though."

"Where do you live?" the dispatcher asked.

Henry gave their home address and explained that

they had been riding to the sheep farm when they discovered the fire.

"I think it is best for you to go home," she said. "I have your address, so emergency responders can find you later if they have questions. It's not safe for you to be near the field."

After Henry hung up, he stood for a few seconds

watching the fire. "I can't believe this! This wind is wild, and the fire is spreading so fast."

Holly gasped, pointing across the field. "The fire is racing across the field toward the forest!"

More smoke was now rising into the sky, high above the trees.

A truck came flying

around the far bend and
skidded to a stop beside
the field. A man jumped
out. It was Mr. Juggins.

"Oh no! Oh no!" he
shouted as he stared in
disbelief at the growing
fire.

Holly and Henry
quickly pedaled over to
Mr. Juggins. They heard
sirens in the distance.

Mr. Juggins pulled out his phone just as the kids reached him, but the elderly man was trembling so much that he dropped the phone in the tall grass.

Holly dropped to her knees and searched the ground. She grabbed the phone and handed it to Mr. Juggins.

"We called 911, Mr. Juggins," Henry said. "I can hear the sirens of the fire trucks in the distance. They will be here very soon."

Mr. Juggins nodded. "Thank you. But this heat and this wind—it's the worst thing for a fire!"

Chapter 3

"Oh, I really want to stay and watch the firefighters," Holly told Henry.

"Me too, Holly, but we need to follow the instructions we were given and go home."

"OK," Holly nodded. Henry called his mom

and explained what had happened, and the siblings pedaled furiously down the trail toward home. Holly said a prayer for Mr. Juggins, whose bee farm was so close to the fire. As they heard sirens getting nearer, they stopped and stood by their bikes. A fire truck flew by them, lights flashing and sirens blaring.

With wonder, Holly watched as two police cars sped by her. It didn't sound like more emergency vehicles were coming.

Glancing over toward the area of the fire, Holly gasped. Huge billows of dark smoke were now rising high into the sky.

"Wow!" Henry

whistled. "I think the fire must've reached the forest behind the field."

As they were putting their bikes in the garage, Holly's dad pulled into the driveway. He often worked from home but had gone into the office today.

"You're home!" Holly called as she ran to her dad and hugged him.

Holly's dog, Snowball, ran around the corner. Holly picked her up.

"Mom called and told me about the fire. I raced home," Dad explained.

The sound of more sirens drew their attention toward the direction of the growing fire. The sky was now filled with smoke.

"I can't believe how much smoke there is. It's scary. Will the fire come here?" Holly asked as they walked toward the house.

"I've been getting updates on my phone as they are posted online," said Holly's mom, who had walked out to join them. "The fire is headed away from us. They are

41

evacuating some areas but not ours."

"Whoa!" Henry shouted, pointing to the sky. "Look at that big plane and how low it is!"

"It's a fire plane," Dad explained excitedly. "And look! Do you see the smaller plane up high in the sky? That plane is getting a good view of the fire, and it will radio that information down to the firefighters, who can't see as well from the ground."

"Is it going to land?" Holly asked.

"No, just watch!" Dad replied.

To Holly's amazement, the larger plane dropped huge amounts of bright red powder out of its belly.

Oh, it's spectacular, Holly thought, watching the white plane against the dark smoke and the misty red powder falling above the green trees.

As the plane flew off, Mom looked down at her phone. "That was fire retardant. They dropped

it on the fields to the east of the fire in case the wind shifts in that direction. The fire can't go backward because it can't burn what has already burned, but if it shifts to the east, it could come back this way. The retardant should stop it."

"What is retardant?" Holly asked.

"It's a substance that

stops or slows down fires,"
Henry explained.

Dad looked at his
phone as well. "A message
just posted. Apparently,
there are many more
houses to the east of the
fire, so the responders are
making sure it doesn't go
that way."

Then Dad frowned.
"Oh dear. This message

says it's too windy for the planes to keep fighting the fire right now. That's not good."

Chapter 4

Holly and her family walked to the garden and sat on the two benches that faced the road.

I'm not surprised the planes can't fly in this wind, Holly thought as her braids whipped in the fierce wind. Occasionally, a police car or a fire truck would zoom by.

"This is a big deal," Mom said. "I wonder how the fire started."

Just then, a police car came around the bend, slowed down, and pulled into the driveway.

"Oh," Henry said. "The 911 dispatcher said that we might be questioned."

Holly was scared, even

though she and Henry hadn't done anything wrong. She had never talked to a police officer.

As the man got out of his car and walked toward them, Holly grabbed her mom's hand.

"Howdy! I'm Officer Howser. Is there a Holly and a Henry here?" asked the young officer.

Holly gulped and raised her hand meekly.

"Yes, that's us," Henry said bravely.

Officer Howser smiled. "Pleased to meet you. Who knows how much more this fire would've spread if you hadn't called 911 when you did? Can I ask you some questions that might help us learn how the fire started?"

Holly nodded, realizing that the officer was kind and helpful.

It didn't take long to answer the officer's questions. Holly and Henry hadn't seen anyone other than Mr. Juggins, and that was after they reported the fire. They didn't see anything else that looked unusual.

"After the fire cools down, and it is safe, can you show us where you first saw the fire? Do you think you would remember?"

Closing her eyes, Holly saw the field in her mind, and she could clearly remember where she first saw flames.

"Yes!" she responded confidently.

"Hopefully, it won't be as windy tomorrow," the

officer said. "We really need air support to fight the fire. I guess the good news is that the wind tends to die down at night."

"Do you think we will need to evacuate?" Dad asked the officer.

"Probably not," the man responded. "The fire has moved several miles farther from where it started a few hours ago. It's moving away from your home, so it's highly unlikely it will come this way."

Holly sighed in relief as the officer started off, but then she had a thought and called out, "Wait! What about Mr. Juggins's home and bee farm that are so close to the fire?"

The officer frowned and hesitated before speaking. "I can't confirm anything for sure yet. Sorry."

Holly's heart dropped.

Mr. Juggins was a very nice man who took care of many honeybees. They had visited the little shop on his property several times and loved his honeycomb ice cream. He always slipped a piece of honey candy into Holly's hand before she left. Mom loved his beeswax candles and honey butter.

"Oh, Mom," Holly said with misty eyes. "I really hope Mr. Juggins and his honeybee farm are OK."

Mom squeezed Holly's hands. "Me too. Why don't we go in and have some lunch, and I'll try to find out?"

Chapter 5

"We have some guests coming to stay with us," Dad said, looking up from his phone.

Holly had just eaten the last bite of her lunch. "Who? Why?" she asked.

"It's the Winter family. I work with Mr. Winter. His family just got evacuated because of the fire. Mom and I invited them to stay with us."

"They have three brand-new pets, so they can't stay at a hotel," Mom explained. "We can keep the new pets in our backyard."

"Pets?" Henry asked. "What kind of pets?"

"You'll see!" Mom said

with a twinkle in her eye.

"How many children do they have?" Holly asked.

"Three—a nine-year-old boy, a seven-year-old girl, and a seventeen-month-old baby girl," Mom replied.

"A baby!" Holly exclaimed. "We don't have a crib or diapers or anything like that."

Mom laughed. "They are bringing a portable crib, and we can get all the diapers and baby food we need at the store."

"They are bringing their trailer," Dad said. "They threw as many of their important things in the trailer as they could . . . just in case."

"In case of what?"

Holly asked.

"In case the fire spreads to their house and it burns down, honey," Mom said.

"Oh," Holly said sadly.

"I'm going to go move my car in front of the barn so there is room for their trailer and two cars," Dad said.

"Why are they bringing two cars?" Holly asked.

"Just in case," Dad said.

"Oh," Holly said quietly. "They don't want to lose their cars if the fire reaches their house."

Mom nodded. "We have another guest coming too."

"Who?" Holly said with wide eyes.

"Mr. Juggins."

"Mr. Juggins!" Holly

burst out. "Oh, of course he has to evacuate—he lives so close to the fire."

Mom looked at Holly with very, very sad eyes. "Holly, Mr. Juggins lost his bee farm. The fire was just too close, and the wind was too strong."

"But the plane!" Holly burst out. "Why didn't it drop that red stuff by his house first?"

"It was already too late," Mom said.

Holly saw a tear slip from her mom's eye.

"I know you don't

know him very well, but I serve with him at the food pantry every Thursday, and we've become friends," Mom explained.

"I felt the Holy Spirit nudge me to contact him and invite him here."

"It turns out he doesn't have any family close by," Dad added. "He didn't have anywhere to go, and he needs a place for his two goats and donkey as well. They can stay in our barn."

"We don't have donkey

or goat food," Holly stated quietly.

"We can get it," Dad said kindly.

Turning toward the window, Holly frowned. Above the trees, she could see large strings of smoke crossing the sky. *I don't like this fire. Not at all. I want Mr. Juggins's bee farm to be OK. I don't want the*

Winters to come here. It is going to be so crowded with strangers and cars and animals.

Holly sighed and got up to help get the house ready for all their new guests.

Chapter 6

Holly moved her clothes
and bedding into her
parents' room and then
helped put clean sheets
and blankets on her bed.

Peeping out the
window, Holly saw that
the Winters had arrived,
and Mr. Juggins was just
pulling his truck and

animal trailer into the
driveway. Mr. and Mrs.
Winter got out of the
car and opened the rear
doors. A toddler and
two older children, all
with straight black hair,
jumped out. The little boy
held an animal carrier.

When Mr. Juggins and
the Winters walked up,
Holly suddenly felt shy.

As she looked at Mr. Juggins, Holly felt like crying. His eyes were full of sadness. Still, he smiled and thanked Holly's family for giving him and his animals a place to stay.

Mr. and Mrs. Winter looked tired but nice.

"I'm Cho," the nine-year-old boy said, shaking Holly's hand.

The seven-year-old girl,
however, hid behind her
mom's skirt, with only

one eye peeping out at Holly.

"That's Ruby," Cho said, pointing to his sister.

Holly's heart went out to the little girl who held tightly to a little suitcase. *Being evacuated from her home must be very scary,* Holly thought.

"You get to stay in my room," Holly said gently

to Ruby. "It has a big window seat and a whole shelf of picture books by it. Do you like to read?"

The girl's other eye appeared from behind her mom's skirt, and she gave a little nod.

"Do you want me to show you?" Holly asked. "And then I can show you Little Glass Lake, and we

can pick flowers to put in
your room." Holly held
out her hand. "Do you

want to come with me?"

The girl nodded again and took Holly's hand, looking at her admiringly.

Holly's heart felt warm. She knew that Ruby had needed her happy, welcoming attitude. Joy filled Holly's heart as she looked over at her mom and saw her mouth the words "thank you."

The visit to Little Glass Lake had to wait, however. Once Ruby was settled into Holly's room, Cho was settled on a cot in the little library, and Mr. and Mrs. Winter were settled in the guest room with their toddler, Holly's dad said they had better get things ready for the Winters' pets.

Oh yeah, Holly thought. *I wonder what the pets are.*

"We just got them this morning," Cho explained. "As soon as we got home from the rabbit farm, we were told we had thirty minutes to evacuate."

Rabbits! Holly thought excitedly. *I love rabbits!*

"We have the panels for the rabbit pen in

the trailer. We wanted to build a nice, big pen for the bunnies to run around in," Mrs. Winter explained. "I hope it doesn't take up too much of your yard."

"There's plenty of room," Mom promised. "We can set them up on the grass. The bunnies will love it."

As the families talked and worked together, they tried to ignore the smell of smoke in the air.

Chapter 7

As soon as the pen was set up, the adults went inside to talk with Mr. Juggins.

Mom came out a few minutes later, looking very sad. "While Mr. Juggins was able to save his donkey and goats, he didn't have time to take anything from his house other than photo albums and his important documents. He needs clothes and . . ." Mom choked up and let out a little sob. "Oh, he needs everything. Dad and Mr. Winter are going to buy him some basic things."

Holly suddenly felt bad that she had not wanted

her house to be crowded. *My house is safe. Mr. Juggins lost so much. I'm glad he can stay here.*

Mom continued, "Henry, I'd love your help making dinner."

"Done!" Henry said as he headed back inside to the kitchen.

"Holly, it would be great if you could play

with Cho and Ruby and help them feel at home."

Holly nodded. "Of course, Mom."

"Thank you, Holly," Mom said. "You have been so much help!"

Holly climbed into the pen with Cho and Ruby.

"They are Netherland Dwarf bunnies," Cho explained.

With delight, Holly watched the three little bunnies hop around and nibble the grass, so happy to be out of their carriers.

"I like the white-and-black one best," Ruby said shyly. "I named it Rose. They are all girls."

"We named the brown one Fern," Cho explained. "And the black one is named Shadow."

"So are they from the Netherlands?" Holly asked.

"Yes, originally, but now people have them as pets all over the world."

"They're one of the smallest kinds of pet rabbits," Ruby shared proudly.

Cho picked up Fern after a few careful tries to catch her. "They don't like being held as much as other kinds of pet rabbits, but they are so soft and cute."

"Can you guess how often we will need to give them a bath?" Ruby asked.

"Once a week?" Holly guessed.

With a shake of her head, Ruby said, "Nope, never. We aren't supposed to bathe them. We read all about this type of rabbit

before we got them."

"Then how do they get clean?" Holly asked.

Ruby giggled. "They groom themselves!"

As if on cue, Rose held up her little paws and started licking them. Then she started licking her fur.

"How cute!" Holly exclaimed.

After several more minutes, the children left the pen. Holly put Snowball on a leash so she could go with them into the oak grove by the house and then to the edge of the yard.

"We are not allowed to go past the grass without Henry or an adult," Holly explained. "But there are

a lot of wildflowers at the
edge of the grass. Why
don't you pick some,

Ruby? We'll put them in your room."

It wasn't long before everyone was back in the house eating a late dinner.

As she ate, Holly gazed out the window at the smoky sunset.

Chapter 8

Just as the police officer had predicted, the wind died down during the night. But it grew in the morning.

After an early breakfast, Mr. Juggins and Mr. and Mrs. Winter sat in the family room, checking updates on the fire.

"Our neighborhood is safe for now, but it might not be if the wind picks back up," Mr. Winter said.

Holly glanced out the window. It was breezy but not as windy as yesterday.

With a troubled face, Ruby kept asking her mom questions about the fire, and Holly could tell that Ruby was feeling anxious.

"Ruby!" Holly said. "I have a guide about rabbits. We could go read it in my tree house!"

That did the trick! Ruby darted over to Holly and held her hand.

After grabbing the *Good and Beautiful Animal Guide* about rabbits from her room, Holly led Ruby and Cho up into the tree house, where the golden light of morning slanted through the leaves. Cho

and Ruby lay on their backs, staring up into the tree while Holly read to them.

Every now and then,

Cho would chime in with information he had learned about Netherland Dwarf bunnies.

"Each day, our rabbits need to eat a pile of hay as big as they are!" Cho said after Holly finished reading the book.

Ruby smiled. "Can you imagine eating a pile of food as big as yourself?"

With a laugh, Holly lay back on the cool wood as well, arms folded behind her head. "That would be very hard to do."

Cho continued, "Hay is actually really important to a rabbit's diet. The fiber in the hay helps move the fur out of their digestive tracts."

"What?" Ruby asked.

"Why do they have fur in their digestive tracts?"

"Oh! I think I know," burst out Holly. "It's because they are always licking their fur, so it gets in their mouths, and they swallow it."

"Probably!" Cho smiled. "They also need so much hay because of their teeth." He turned to

Ruby. "Did you know that unlike our teeth, which don't keep growing, rabbit teeth never stop growing?"

"Wow," Ruby whispered.

Turning his head back to look up into the tree, Cho continued, "Chewing so much hay helps keep their teeth worn down. If they didn't keep wearing down, imagine how much they would grow and what trouble that would cause."

Ruby gasped softly. "They could get as long as a pencil!"

"I don't know if that would make me scream or laugh!" Holly declared.

Cho and Ruby broke out into a fit of laughter. Mingled with the laughter was a low rumble. The wood in the tree house started to vibrate.

Suddenly, everyone stopped laughing and sat up. The tree house started shaking, and a loud, deep rumble filled the air.

Ruby scooted over to Cho and held onto him. "Oh! Is it an earthquake?"

Holly was scared too. Nothing like this had ever happened before.

The deep sound got louder and louder.

Chapter 9

The three children crawled toward the huge tree trunk in the center of the tree house. Huddled against the sturdy trunk, they clamped their hands over their ears.

I've never heard anything so loud, Holly thought in alarm.

A strong wind slammed into Holly's face and swished the leaves around

loudly. She wanted to ask Cho what he thought was going on, but it was just too loud.

When it seemed the noise couldn't get any louder, Holly noticed a shadow fall over the tree house. Looking up, she saw a huge metal object moving slowly. Finally, she realized what it was.

A helicopter! she thought. *What is a helicopter doing here?*

Then she saw the

bucket hanging from the helicopter. *It's going to get water from Little Glass Lake to help fight the fire!*

The children watched as the helicopter hovered over the lake, slowly going down until the huge bucket splashed into the lake and sank out of sight.

This is so amazing, Holly thought, even though she

was still a little scared.

Soon, the bucket lifted out of the water, and the helicopter zoomed

away, the dripping bucket swinging below it.

As the sound faded into the distance, Holly, Cho, and Ruby started chattering as they quickly climbed down from the tree house.

The adults and Henry were all standing on the back porch.

"Did you see that?" Holly exclaimed as she ran up to them.

"Yes! It was so neat," Mom answered. "I hope you weren't too scared."

"Oh, I was scared!" Holly laughed. "But I'm OK. It was so exciting to see it up close!"

"It will probably come back again," Mom said.

"Oh! I bet the bunnies are so scared," Ruby said suddenly.

"Let's go check on them," Cho said. "Come on, Holly!"

Chapter 10

When they reached the bunny pen, they didn't see any bunnies hopping around the grass.

"Are they in the little hutch?" Cho asked.

They got into the pen and opened the roof of the hutch.

Holly's eyes widened.

She saw the white bunny
with black spots and the
brown bunny, but the
black one was not there.

"Shadow is missing!"
Ruby hollered so loudly

that the adults heard and came over.

"How could that be?" Mr. Winter wondered, inspecting the pen. "There are no gaps in the pen that she could've gone through."

Mrs. Winter checked all around the bottom of the pen. "There are no gaps at all at the bottom."

"Maybe she jumped over the pen?" Ruby suggested.

Cho shook his head. "I read that some Netherland Dwarf bunnies can hop as high as three feet, but this pen is four feet high."

"Maybe Shadow is a super jumper!" Ruby said, making up the term.

"I really don't think she

could jump that high," Mrs. Winter said. "But I hope she has not gotten far. We might not be able to find her again if she has gone off into the woods."

Ruby sniffed, her eyes misty.

"It's OK!" Holly said, taking Ruby's hand. "Let's all look for her."

Everyone jumped into

action, checking under the porch, behind the bushes, and in the garden.

"Here she is!" Henry called. "She is eating vegetables in the garden." But as Henry reached to grab her, she jumped away toward Mr. Juggins. He reached for the bunny as she flew past, but he missed her too!

For several minutes
everyone tried to catch
her. Finally, Mr. Juggins
slowly crept up behind
the bunny as she stopped

to eat a dandelion. He
scooped her up carefully
in his hands and held her
close to his chest.

"Phew!" Holly said.

A rumble in the distance sounded.

"The helicopter is coming back," Cho said, pointing to the sky. "Let's hurry and get Shadow back into the hutch."

Most of the morning and into early afternoon, the group sat on the back porch, reading updates online about the fire and

watching the helicopter
scoop up water from Little
Glass Lake.

"They were able to keep
the fire away from the
sheep farm!" Mom said
cheerfully.

"Yay!" Holly burst out.
But then she saw a sad
look on Mr. Juggins's face,
so she went to sit by him.

For an hour, Holly and

Mr. Juggins talked. Holly learned all about him and his love for bees. His wife had died a few years ago. They had one child who had died as a young adult.

"That is one reason I loved my shop," Mr. Juggins said. "All the friendly people who visited every day kept me busy and not so lonely."

"What will you do now?" Holly asked.

"I'm not sure," Mr. Juggins responded. "But there is one thing I do know—when we are faithful, God takes care of us. That doesn't mean life isn't hard sometimes, but I feel Him with me."

Mr. Winter suddenly jumped up. "Great news!

The wind has totally died down, and they have the fire ninety-nine percent contained. Our house is going to be safe!"

"That *is* great news," Holly said. Then she looked at Mr. Juggins. "But I'm so sorry about your farm."

Mr. Juggins smiled. "See how God is helping

me? What better place could I be than with friends on this beautiful piece of land?"

"It is an amazing lake," Holly stated. "Do you want to walk around it? I can show you some neat things."

Mr. Juggins nodded.

Chapter 11

As Holly, Mr. Juggins, and Henry walked around the lake, swallows swooped across the fields, squirrels ran along the tree limbs, and yellow butterflies fluttered here and there. The clouds floated lazily in the blue sky.

"This really is a little
piece of heaven here!"

Mr. Juggins sighed.

Just then, Holly heard voices. She turned and saw some strangers on Gabe's land, talking to a man holding a black folder. With the adults stood a teenage girl. She was glued to her phone.

Gabe was running across the field toward Holly, waving.

Out of breath, Gabe reached Holly and explained who the strangers were. "They're looking at the land to see if they want to buy it."

"Oh," Holly said, looking at the teenager, who glanced around, frowned, and turned her attention back to her phone.

I don't want new neighbors, Holly thought to herself.

Back at the house, Holly learned that Shadow had gone missing from the pen again and was found in the garden.

"We caught her faster this time," Cho explained, "but we can't figure out how she keeps escaping."

The children carefully checked the pen and could not find any gaps in or underneath the pen.

"It's a mystery!" Cho shrugged.

"Let's hide behind those bushes," Holly said. "Then we can see how Shadow is getting out."

"Great idea!" Cho agreed, and they made

themselves comfortable
behind some bushes a few
feet from the pen.

"Are bunnies

nocturnal?" Holly asked Cho quietly as they waited.

"Not exactly," Cho responded. "They sleep just during the darkest part of night and also the brightest part of day. So they are most active at dawn and dusk."

"Look!" Ruby whispered. "Shadow is

standing up on her hind legs and reaching her front legs up on the pen."

"What is she doing?" Cho wondered.

Then, to the astonishment of the children, the rabbit skillfully climbed the pen as if it were a ladder. When she got near the top, she pushed off with her powerful legs and jumped out of the pen. "What?" Cho shouted

as he stood up. "Bunnies can't climb!"

"That one can!" Holly laughed. "She's not a super jumper—she's a super *climber!*"

As the children laughed and squealed, they worked together to return the bunny to the hutch.

"Let's go tell my parents!" Cho suggested.

Inside, they found Mr. and Mrs. Winter packing.

"We are able to go home this evening!" they explained happily.

The doorbell rang. It was a police officer, asking if Holly and Henry could come show him where they had first seen the fire.

Mr. Juggins got in the minivan with Holly

and her family. Since it
was now safe to go to his
farm, he wanted to see the
damage.

At the field, Holly
and Henry pointed to
the place where they
remembered first seeing
the fire, and investigators
headed toward that area.

"Let's stay here and
watch them while Dad

takes Mr. Juggins to his land," Mom suggested.

Holly was glad about that. She wanted to watch the investigators, and she thought it would be too sad to see Mr. Juggins's burned home and land.

When the men returned, Mr. Juggins's eyes were red. Holly felt so sad for him. Mr. Juggins had come to mean a lot to her in the short time he had been with her family.

A police officer walked toward them. "Well, it wasn't too hard to figure out what probably started the fire." He held up a broken glass bottle. "Someone likely threw this bottle out their window. Glass containers can act like a magnifying glass, creating a ray of light so hot it can catch this dry grass on fire. Then a hot, windy day can make the little flames grow rapidly."

Chapter 12

After dinner, the
Winters left.

I'll miss Cho and Ruby,
Holly thought as she got
in bed that night. *I'll miss
the rabbits too!*

Holly lay in her bed
reading, and then she
stared at the starry sky
out her window. Her

thoughts jumped around to the Winter family, Mr. Juggins, and the fire.

Holly's dad came in and knelt by her bed.

"I came to say good night."

"I was thinking," Holly started, looking at her dad, "that whoever threw that bottle into the field caused the fire and caused Mr. Juggins's bee farm to burn down."

Dad nodded. "Yes, that's true. It's very sad."

"What is Mr. Juggins

going to do, Dad?"

"I'm not sure, honey. But we have told him that he can stay here until he figures it out."

"Good!" Holly smiled as she snuggled down into her blanket.

Three days later, Holly and Henry decided to ride their bikes to Faith's house. Faith had just gotten back from her camp—the one Holly had been able to pay for with the money from the hummingbird picture.

At the end of the driveway, Holly looked left down the street.

"Look, Henry!" Holly said. "The For Sale sign isn't there anymore."

"Maybe Gabe's family

decided not to sell their land!" Henry suggested.

"I hope so!" Holly sang as they started toward Faith's house.

Later that evening, back at home, Holly's mom was just finishing dinner. "Holly, can you tell Mr. Juggins it's time to eat?" she asked.

"Sure, where is he?"

"Outside in the back."

Holly skipped outside.
The sun was sinking
low in the sky, sending
slanting sunbeams
through breaks in the
huge piles of clouds.

Holly stood in the
middle of the grass in the
backyard, looking around.
Squinting, she saw Mr.
Juggins standing on top

of a small hill in the field that belonged to Gabe's family.

Since it was too far to call to him, Holly jogged over to the hill.

Mr. Juggins waved as Holly got closer and motioned her to come to where he was. When she reached him, he smiled. "The lake is so

beautiful from this spot. I think I'll build my house here."

"Your house?" Holly burst out. "But this land belongs to Gabe's family."

Mr. Juggins shook his head. "Not for much longer. I made an offer on it today, and it was accepted. What do you think of having a bee

farmer as your new
neighbor?"

Holly pressed her
hands together in
excitement.

"You, our neighbor? Oh, I couldn't be more excited!"

The world around them seemed to be excited too. Little Glass Lake sparkled, the birds sang, and the flowers nodded in the breeze as if saying, "Yes, we agree."

Try another Level 2B book from The Good and the Beautiful.

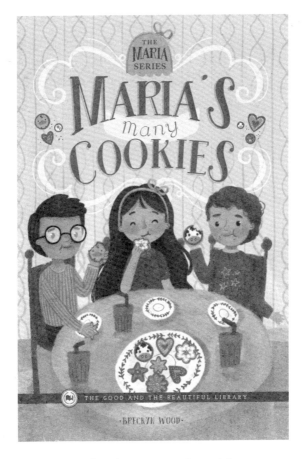

Maria's Many Cookies
By Breckyn Wood

goodandbeautiful.com